Animals grow and change

Bobbie Kalman

 Crabtree Publishing Company

www.crabtreebooks.com

Created by Bobbie Kalman

Dedicated by Samantha Crabtree
To Chanelle Coleman Selman

**Author and
Editor-in-Chief**
Bobbie Kalman

Editors
Reagan Miller
Robin Johnson

Photo research
Crystal Sikkens

Design
Bobbie Kalman
Katherine Berti
Samantha Crabtree (cover)

Production coordinator
Katherine Berti

Illustrations
Barbara Bedell: pages 8, 24 (kangaroo nursing)
Anne Giffard: page 16
Bonna Rouse: pages 1 (top left and middle butterflies), 24 (bird life cycle
    and turtle hatching)
Margaret Amy Salter: pages 1 (all except top left and middle butterflies),
    20, 23, 24 (caterpillar)

Photographs
© iStockphoto.com: pages 5 (bottom), 17 (top), 19 (tadpoles), 24 (tadpole)
© 2008 Jupiterimages Corporation: pages 10, 11, 16
© ShutterStock.com: pages 1, 3, 4, 5 (top), 6, 7, 8, 9, 12, 13, 14, 15, 17 (bottom),
    18, 19 (eggs and frogs), 20, 21, 22, 23, 24 (rat, butterfly, chick, and cat)
Other images by Corel

Library and Archives Canada Cataloguing in Publication

Kalman, Bobbie, 1947-
    Animals grow and change / Bobbie Kalman.

(Introducing living things)
Includes index.
ISBN 978-0-7787-3227-3 (bound).--ISBN 978-0-7787-3251-8 (pbk.)

    1. Animal life cycles--Juvenile literature. 2. Growth--Juvenile
literature. I. Title. II. Series.

QL49.K329 2007   j571.8'1   C2007-904698-3

The Library of Congress has cataloged the printed edition as follows:
Kalman, Bobbie.
    Animals grow and change / Bobbie Kalman.
        p. cm. -- (Introducing living things)
    Includes index.
    ISBN-13: 978-0-7787-3227-3 (rlb)
    ISBN-10: 0-7787-3227-4 (rlb)
    ISBN-13: 978-0-7787-3251-8 (pb)
    ISBN-10: 0-7787-3251-7 (pb)
    1. Animals--Juvenile literature. 2. Growth--Juvenile literature. I. Title.
II. Series.

QL49.K293 2007
590--dc22
                                                    2007030176

Crabtree Publishing Company
www.crabtreebooks.com   1-800-387-7650

Printed in the U.S.A./022013/SN20130115

**Published in Canada
Crabtree Publishing**
616 Welland Ave.
St. Catharines, Ontario
L2M 5V6

**Published in the United States
Crabtree Publishing**
PMB 59051
350 Fifth Avenue, 59th Floor
New York, New York 10118

**Published in the United Kingdom
Crabtree Publishing**
Maritime House
Basin Road North, Hove
BN41 1WR

**Published in Australia
Crabtree Publishing**
3 Charles Street
Coburg North
VIC, 3058

Contents

Born or hatch?

Animals are living things. Living things grow and change. Some animals begin their lives growing inside the bodies of their mothers. The animals are then **born**. These lambs were just born. The mother sheep is cleaning one of the lambs.

Some baby animals do not grow inside their mothers' bodies. Their mothers **lay** eggs. The babies grow inside the eggs, and then they **hatch**. To hatch is to break out of an egg. This swan has laid some eggs.

These baby birds have just hatched from their eggs.

Mammals are born

Most **mammals** are born. Mammals are animals with hair or fur on their bodies. Some mammal babies are born without hair or fur. The baby rats above will grow fur. They will soon look like the rat on the left.

Mammal mothers make milk in their bodies. Their babies drink the milk. Drinking mother's milk is called **nursing**. These kittens and puppies are nursing.

Pocket babies

Some mammal babies are tiny when they are born. **Marsupials** are mammals that have tiny babies. Kangaroos and koalas are marsupials.

kangaroo joey nursing

Most marsupial mothers have **pouches**, or pockets, on their bodies. After they are born, marsupial babies live in their mothers' pouches. The **joeys**, or babies, nurse inside the pouches. This kangaroo joey is sleeping inside its mother's pouch.

Joeys spend a lot of time in their mothers' pouches. As they grow, the joeys start spending time out of the pouches. They stay close to their mothers. The joeys start to eat grasses and other foods. They nurse, as well.

Mother's care

Mammal mothers feed their babies and hide them from **predators**. Predators are animals that hunt and eat other animals. Mammal mothers move their babies when they think the babies are in danger. This cougar mother is carrying her **cub** to a new hiding place. She is not hurting it. All cats carry their babies by the **scruff**, or back of the neck.

Mammal mothers teach their babies how to find food and how to move from place to place. The orangutan mother above is swinging from tree to tree. Her baby hangs on to her chest. As the baby grows, it will climb and swing on its own.

What is a life cycle?

Animals are born, or they hatch. As they grow, their bodies change on the outside and on the inside. The changes an animal goes through are called its **life cycle**. The life cycle of a horse starts when a **foal**, or baby horse, is born. This foal was just born.

Foals stand soon after they are born. The foal's mother is helping it stand up.

A horse's life cycle

A horse is a mammal.
Mammal babies nurse as
soon as they are born. They
look a lot like their parents.

Fully grown horses are **adults**.
Adults can make babies. This horse
is carrying a baby inside her body. A
new life cycle starts with every baby.

Foals nurse and start eating
grass, too. They grow quickly.
One foal is nursing, and the
other is eating grass.

Hatching birds

The life cycles of birds start with eggs. A mother bird lays eggs. **Chicks**, or baby birds, hatch from the eggs. Most mother birds care for their chicks. Some father birds also help care for their chicks.

These pictures show a chick hatching from an egg.

1

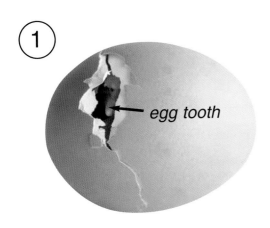

The baby bird cracks the egg with its **egg tooth**.

2

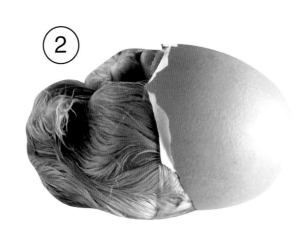

It starts to push out of the shell. Hatching is hard work!

3

The baby bird is now out of the shell. Its feathers are wet.

4

When the feathers dry, they are soft and fuzzy.

15

Reptile changes

Snakes, lizards, alligators, and turtles belong to a group of animals called **reptiles**. Most reptiles hatch from eggs. Reptile mothers lay soft eggs. These baby snakes are breaking out of their soft eggs. Baby snakes look just like their mothers, but they are smaller.

Reptile mothers do not care for their eggs or babies. The mothers lay their eggs and leave. Baby sea turtles hatch on their own and find their way to the ocean, where they will live.

Lizards also look like their parents when they hatch. This picture shows a family of bearded dragons. When lizards become adults, they can make babies.

baby

young

adult

Big frog changes

Some animals go through big changes as they grow. They start their lives in eggs. Their bodies change many times before they become adults. These big changes are called **metamorphosis**. All frogs start their lives in water. All frogs go through metamorphosis. This water is full of frog eggs.

A frog's life cycle

A new life cycle starts with every egg that hatches.

A tadpole hatches from an egg. It has a tail for swimming.

*A female frog lays many eggs in water. Frog eggs are called **spawn**.*

The tadpole soon grows back legs.

The adult frog can live on land and in water. It can make babies.

The tadpole has become a young frog. It has lost its tail and can breathe air.

Monarch caterpillar

Butterflies also go through metamorphosis. Butterflies start their lives inside eggs. Caterpillars hatch from the eggs. These caterpillars are hatching from eggs.

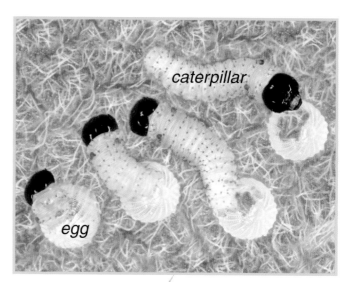

caterpillar

egg

old skin

Caterpillars eat and eat. They grow and grow. As they grow, they get too big for their skin. Caterpillars lose their old skin and grow new skin. Losing old skin and growing new skin is called **molting**. Caterpillars molt many times.

The caterpillar then hangs upside down and makes a hard case around its body. It is now a **pupa**. Its case is called a **chrysalis**. The caterpillar's body changes inside the chrysalis. What happens next? Turn the page!

pupa

chrysalis

A new butterfly

The chrysalis becomes clear. You can
see the butterfly inside. The new butterfly
breaks out of the chrysalis. The butterfly's
wings are still wet. It cannot fly yet.

When its wings are dry, the butterfly can fly away. Soon, the butterfly can lay eggs. The eggs will grow into new caterpillars and butterflies.

eggs

Words to know and Index

baby rat

born
pages 4, 6,
8, 12, 13

butterfly
pages 20,
22, 23

caterpillar
pages 20,
21, 23

egg *chick*

hatching
pages 4, 5, 12, 14,
15, 16, 17, 19, 20

life cycle
pages 12,
13, 14, 19

mammals
pages 6, 7, 8,
10, 11, 13

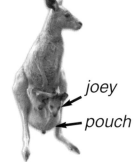
joey *pouch*

marsupials
pages 8-9

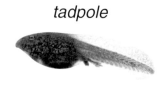
tadpole

metamorphosis
pages 18, 20

kangaroo

nursing
pages 7, 8, 9, 13

turtle hatching

reptiles
pages 16-17